CIRCLE BACK

Also by Adam Clay

To Make Room for the Sea
Stranger
A Hotel Lobby at the Edge of the World
The Wash

CIRCLE BACK

poems

Adam Clay

MILKWEED EDITIONS

Published 2024 by Milkweed Editions
Printed in the United States of America
Cover design by Mary Austin Speaker
Cover artwork by Etel Adnan
24 25 26 27 28   5 4 3 2 1
First Edition

Library of Congress Cataloging-in-Publication Data

Names: Clay, Adam, 1978- author.
Title: Circle back : poems / Adam Clay.
Description: First edition. | Minneapolis, Minnesota : Milkweed
Editions, 2024. | Summary: "An aching meditation on the cyclical
nature of grief and memory's limited capacity to preserve everything time
takes from us."-- Provided by publisher.
Identifiers: LCCN 2023030343 (print) | LCCN 2023030344 (ebook) | ISBN
9781639550982 (trade paperback) | ISBN 9781639550999 (ebook)
Subjects: LCGFT: Poetry.
Classification: LCC PS3603.L385 C57 2024 (print) | LCC PS3603.L385
(ebook) | DDC 811/.6--dc23/eng/20230720
LC record available at https://lccn.loc.gov/2023030343
LC ebook record available at https://lccn.loc.gov/2023030344

Milkweed Editions is committed to ecological stewardship. We strive to align our book
production practices with this principle, and to reduce the impact of our operations in
the environment. We are a member of the Green Press Initiative, a nonprofit coalition of
publishers, manufacturers, and authors working to protect the world's endangered forests
and conserve natural resources. Circle Back was printed on acid-free
30% postconsumer-waste paper by Versa Press.

Contents

3.

you try to write faster than the thread is pulled

—W.S. Merwin

We are done for
in the most remarkable ways.

—Brigit Pegeen Kelly

CIRCLE BACK

What Forks Will Splinter Probability

The architect wants the story not born yet.

—Matthew Henriksen

I can still see the deer blood
on the fence and the bone shards
in the drive. The blooms
on the trees held back. Had I
not known the deer was euthanized,
the narrative would have been
charted in the sky
for days or weeks to come.
A story gaps the river. Like how
I mistook myself for myself,
a mirror finds its edges
by tracing what can't be held.
Think of a memorial to stone
in an endless field of gravel. I kept
thinking my life had sharpened down
to what's surer than a point. But
what to do with the dust of April
in the wake of a year meant to end all
those to come? I know it was May when
I wrote these words—now it's months
later, but time feels like a storm shadow,
like something new on the horizon.
On the bookshelf there's some pattern
of life emerging and then suddenly
on the top shelf, ash in a box,

and I am surprised by how weight
repositions form into content, content
into a desk drawer. Everything
last touched by the dead somehow
feels sacred or holy. The inside
of a rock unseen. What to touch
and what to be left as it was?
Astro Black, side A. What's half
a life lived or cradled in temporary
light? My sense of memory
always out to pasture. Should
the narrative I recall
collect rainwater? Some coastal
storm miles inland. Another day
fragmented by stops and starts.

*

Perhaps it's time to trace the body
out each morning as if
it's already gone. Senseless
blooming ahead of a season's
turn. Some version of the world
over there in the magnolias
draped in snow. Another tree
down in the creek swollen
from last year's storm. I don't
need to know what's happened
to know what's to come.
All perspective is glossed with want,

desire colored by some deeper
urge to live on and on. The longer
I decide on each breath, the more
I feel unsure of multitudes
within a life. It's all the same,
how we spin through time,
how we think about a life
digital, a life blurred by
perspectives dulled to a point.

*

Some sledgehammers find
their way to the source of thought,
while others hit the ground,
leave an oyster-shell mark
in the concrete. Will the bruise
still be there when I'm not?

*

I don't doubt reincarnation,
or rather I don't doubt
something larger beyond
the clouds, something calling
my name to make me look
away. So much left to say
to my daughter in this life—
the thunderstorms of December
make me feel more alive

than the glare of the sun
in the thick promise
of spring. I sleep too long,
and I sleep some more.
At some point I feel like saying
anything—even nonsense—
should frame each breath
eternally. Sun Ra up loud
from the other room—what
haunts one of us would
haunt anyone.

*

Months later or earlier perhaps
and rerouted past a wildfire
in Wichita Falls, my daughter
and I out West briefly
and thinking about what
the beginning of the end
will look like. I can't help
but wonder if this is it. I wonder
where language will fail us. The heat
of the prairie wind I can still
feel on my face.

*

Love is an evolving storm
turning roofs into wreckage, fragments
into whole parts. We slowed
behind a tractor trailer, the cows,
as the traffic crawled, looked
at us with the wisdom and grief
of an earlier time. It could flood
or it could never rain again,
their eyes remaining unchanged.
The river we crossed on Saturday
somehow dried up on Tuesday.
I closed my eyes and imagined
the grayness of the sky
and the radical optimism of birth
while the trees fall
around us. *To fell* feels wrong
to say like rope to a belltower
could be more accurate in a world
traced from pine to delta to grassland
to desert to mountains and back again.

*

Most coincidences come to light
to illuminate the space we hold as somehow
delicate or unique. The mind
has always craved order
like a pear tree bloom
past the prime of the fruit. On
Lafayette Street that summer Matt

and I read Larkin with Whitehead
and stumbled over what a life
can mean or be. Like on
what side of the train
is the passenger sitting in "The Whitsun
Weddings." I still read the ending
of "An Arundel Tomb"
through a dark glass. Some other
moments surface to light. The sprinkler
I dashed through after turning my paper in.
Call me when you get to where you're going. The water
droplets on Jim's shirt as he followed
me out, walking through the sprinkler.
I write to depollute what I won't forget.

*

We stay anchored to the world
long enough to hold back
rivers that want to run through
us. In this late year of our survival,
how not to be sincere? There
are enough impulses to slip
through on a daily basis. In all
honesty, I've tried other forms
of placing fashioned thoughts
into chaos lit up as if by two
stones smashed together. As if
I've been speaking this sentence
since I could speak.

*

In the church again I didn't expect
my breath to leave me. I wake up
in Greenpoint some mornings
until my mind shakes loose the leaves
left up for nothing. A season skipped
with no one worried or wondering
why. Our expectations unspool
like some word you can't say
but you keep trying anyhow.

*

My daddy lives there
he says as we drive past
the bookshop,
a place built for holding
many lives. What we
haunt once haunted us.
The obvious wind unlocks
the back door while
Whatever I have to do has not yet begun
feels like a door slamming shut.
No need for finality. I feel
so deeply all of the things
I can't stand to show, tell
my daughter that grief sorts
its parts out regardless

of what we feel on the surface
of the water. A storm on the horizon
stirs everyone the same way.

*

Nothing's where it should be.
I realize this is my fault, largely.
It's unintentional.
Like how a moment's bookended between all others.
Until someone corrects my memory.
The cemetery shouldn't be here.
But I blink my eyes.
And it's still there.
I am always running a circle around it.

1.

Black-Capped Chickadee: Original Motion Picture Soundtrack

—after Tracy K. Smith

I hear its song before I notice its coloring,
know its place in the forest before
it knows I'm here unless
my ear's just dragging something
larger from the sky to my brain
seeking sense. Whatever
burns out can also sing out. It makes
a noise I stir like a fire, audible
as the color of chalk or a thought
that taunts dully before sleep. Because
they fly, the birds strike borders
in the sky we can't see. I'll return
to this moment later in life dozens
of times. The heat of the day
gristles and glistens to light.

Some Mood

The kids at the park light a kite
on fire and watch it lift into the sky,
while back home later, everything I
touch feels like overripe fruit
right before it breaks open. This
is some mood to have. For how many
years will I gloss over words, drop
ice into a glass, count the number of trees
on this lot in case something's changed
overnight? No clouds on the skyline,
the sunlight awful and brutal.
A motorcycle rips the day open
with its wretched and intentional sound.

Shared Custody

We lean hard into spring,
knowing time, weather,
and all else will eventually break
like a clock. My daughter's
grown an inch since
last Monday. We leash the dog,
knowing a walk through
the neighborhood to be a good place
to vent into the sky. She apologizes,
but it's all formality colored
by age. Funny how the community
cats seem to be under a spell
when we approach—they zigzag
down the sidewalk and through
the uncut yards of clover
to rest beneath her hand. Under
these paved avenues lie bricks
waiting to be brought up
to the sun. I imagine the ocean
that once was here and will be
again. Everything I say matters,
like sawing a saw in two.

Poem for a Pandemic

We all say *we're doing the best*
we can and laugh knowing
it isn't true. But we keep saying it,
emphasizing a different word every time
we lob a battery into the ocean, broken
appliance parts into a time capsule
for whoever will find what we leave behind.
We're strangely optimistic. We're
doing the best we can. My watch
tells me to move around. Someone
else's watch tells them to breathe.
I slouch. I stand up straight.
The mirrors ghost us into another
world. Yesterday I looked tired,
but today it's a new type
of yawning, something
fundamental to our existence
yet somehow more ominous. We're doing
the *best* we can. Like something
moving under the skin. Like
skin feeling almost artificial. I wake
up and can't shake the feeling
of sleep. I fill a bowl with cereal
past the capacity of the bowl.

Aesthetic

Jotting down details
of a day to keep
it with me,
when by noon
my hand breaks
down to stone.
Earlier, my daughter
dropped the phrase
dark academia into
an aside. That's enough
for today. I flip
the record but don't
listen to the other side.

Elegy for a Town Built by Trains

I wonder: a life runs
parallel to what,
exactly? Seeing an owl
that morning in the orchard
stunned me from me.
Actually, there
was no orchard, just
the heart-jump and the bird
scattered into an image
I piece together from
memory now.
It was the branch
of a walnut outside
the room where I sleep.
I live in a town built
by trains, knowing every
place one day becomes
an elegy for itself. The first
thing to go after the trains:
the trees. Shortly after,
the undergrowth found
its way here like never before.
How strange that the heart
wants so much and then
will simply stop one day.

Where Paradise Lay

—for John Prine

I posit my body
on the edge
of sorrow
differently today.
The sun follows
the call of a bird
like how last week
you heard everything
I thought before
I said it, heard
the air smelled
like snakes the last
time it was sung
before he sang it,
and we cut the road
open with the car
and a clear
grip on the future
and each of its stars.

Best Wishes

I arrive with belongings
that make little sense:
a buzz saw
for the garden,
irises to be planted
in the long grunt of winter,
and a tall clear glass
with the bottom
cut out. What we
carry becomes a type
of wreckage to hold
a memory down.
Everything ends up
reframed into true
or false questions,
but the act of asking
means more than the end
result. Alright, we are doing
things half-right. If there's
a book that records my
mistakes, I hope you will have
time to eat its pages before
I make my way
to the heaven that's been
left just perfect enough
to disrupt.

Two Sides of the Same Coin

I've heard of both a factory of birds
and a foundling museum the past few days
and they shuffle around in the air;
where one begins and the other ends, I can't
know. I thought the birds were flying
into the smokestacks, but looking back now,
I realize it was the factory spitting them
out. On Friday I saw the sun setting
into the lake; this morning driving north
on my right past Bogue Chitto, it looked less
magnificent, a lamp someone forgot to put out.

Strange Belonging

Here's a neighborhood made up
of every house you've ever lived in.
Your parents driving home from
the hospital. Some of the houses
you don't recognize. The shrubs
of the mind hide both past and future
with such strange belonging. Some
dog you've never seen before. A memory
you'll have one day illuminates
the streetlights. They glow
so bright they're visible from space.

The Great Indifference

From the desert we plucked cactus needles
during the day to play 78s all night long.
The records didn't get dusty or scratched.
We folded books into swans, and swans
into last-minute excuses to stay in,
sleep it off. What we were sleeping off,
we couldn't say or know. We did what
we were told, but it was always a bit sideways
from sense. I didn't think absence would be
the thing I would miss the most, but I did,
I do, and I always will. From inland the ocean
almost makes me feel things I've never felt before.

Ecocriticism

Like a crow I crossed
the country gathering
pieces of myself
to set in the sand. Either
the body has limits
or the twine gets cut. Take
a nap in the gray space
and maybe not wake up,
maybe walk a mile
in shoes not meant
for the terrain you've walked
for so long. Two roads
do away with most other
questions. I've always
admired the rain's persistence
and how the tree, and all
trees, become sharper
in the light of today.

After Listening to a Podcast About Nuclear Tactical Weapons, I Go Outside to Take In the Sunrise

Summer blurs like honey
on the back of your hand. Those
who feel inevitable are usually
most unsure of themselves. I doubt
the world beyond my door
until I think of the bug
on its back in the tub,
its twenty-four hours of living
some kind of dashed-off
lifetime. Everything dangerous
feels silent and strong. I scroll
through memories, remember
a thousand things that, without
my phone, I would surely forget.
I cross the street without
looking either way.

A Year of Dreams Without Birds

The patterned light lines
my sleeping face. Like
a heaven to hitch the day to,
I add a thunderbolt
to the public domain,
hammer out the self
as a child for fear
of losing the few
memories banked
up. Where
are the mid-80s?
A wagon rolls
into the street. I grip
the pinecone so tight
in the past, my hand
turns red in the present.
I broom up every
stream I've ever crossed.

Finishing Another Book About the World Coming to an End

When I say drought, I mean to say
it will rain one day. On the other side
of the globe, a lake appears where
there wasn't one before. I hear
"honesty is a hindrance
when you want to be what's true"
across the unharvested fields with crops
only cut from the wind. Barbed wire
like boredom on the highway. There's
no verb for every action. You can't help
what you feel, but you can feel what
you can't help. Once I wrote an essay
in an afternoon and a week later discovered
I had written the same exact essay
two years before. The children at the park
speak their own language. If we left them
alone for a few more years, I wonder
what wonder they'd stumble upon.

The Bar in Fayetteville Where All the Moms Now Drink

There was a thread I followed
in the quiet of the early aughts
thinking that a proximity to death
could illuminate something
about art I couldn't understand
otherwise. Perhaps I wanted to fix
what wasn't broken or wanted to break
what didn't need repair. I didn't
know at the time why the cemetery
felt so pristine. I didn't know
why darkness was the only distance
my eyes could adjust to. Now I see
mothers in the late afternoon light
sitting at the same tables we once
haunted. Even now, I can see Matt
shooting pool, looking like a muscle
of trouble that could never unravel
no matter how hard one might pull.

2.

Framed by the Screen

In the dull thud of that year,
my therapist asked: *how does*
running so much make you feel?
and in the time of washing clothes
just to put them back on, I answered
as if filled with a ghost: *like an arrow*
being shot from a quiver into stone.

Darkling I Listen

A professor once mentioned as an aside
that there are lines in "Ode to a Nightingale"
written to mimic the bird's call. Maybe
he was right or maybe he wasn't—either way
the class spent a stretch looking, listening,
mouthing the stressed and unstressed
words on the page. On Keats' poem,
a critic writes that "lyric is thus a mode
that simultaneously erases and expresses
selfhood." I think of an eraser and a pencil
working alongside each other. Part of me
can't help but think Keats called
the birdsong "immortal" because
of his poem and not the Romantic idea that nature,
through its cycles and turns, will ebb and flow
forever. Sometimes the ego's optimism
remains beautiful even when it's utterly
and completely flawed. I'd rather think of Keats,
sketching himself back into place. On
the Golden Record that's out of the solar system
now, scientists deemed the sound of birds
important enough to include as a marker
of our planet. Listening this morning to a clip
of what someone or something might hear one day,
I can't help but wonder if they'll
even know what it is. Maybe they'll think
it was the language we spoke to one another

to say what we longed for, the language
we used to say one day when I'm gone,
and you're out among the trees,
please, please remember me.

Adam Clay

He didn't want the early morning
dream to end so he stayed asleep all day,
eyes closed at work and in the car
on the way to and from. No one
questions madness in the form
of a routine, but routine
madness is another thing altogether.
No one was in the dream except for
himself at every single age of his life.
A father holding himself as a child.
A child comforting an older, confused,
and drifting version of himself. There
was a breeze just outside the door
but no breeze in the breezeway.

Mixtape Archive Circa 1997

The sun like a hubcap through the clouds
because coarse light emerges from
so many places. Some scratchy guitar solo
disappears inside a wrecked piano, later
tossed to sea. A thought skips ahead,
plays out, pauses, starts again: searching
the cassette for some familiar strain.
I dreamt the middle of the boulevard
was fragmented into gravel and dust,
and sure enough it happened
the next day. From that decade
the silence between the songs, it turns out,
was all today I needed to hear.

Iowa Workshop Model

—for F.

In the city of churches,
I looked up always
for no good reason and looked
down at the ants piled
on top of each other, found no
metaphor apt enough
for the literal light of
day. Give a poet
a suitcase of cash at sunset,
and the suitcase will be
missing by dawn. Once a phone
rang in the classroom,
but no one owned up to forgetting
to silence. Finally the professor
stopped class, pretended to pick it up,
said hello, paused, and promptly
hung up, his finger smudging
the imaginary button. *It was my father,*
he said. Outside it was fall,
yet the cherry trees outside
were just beginning to bloom.

Imposter Syndrome While Isolating at Home

A colliding cocktail of love
and grief. I hold off on
the Joni Mitchell ascension
stream until I'm alone for a week
or maybe two. Like a weighted blanket,
the sky hangs, its sentence
stretching out far beyond
what the mind allows. I took a jar
of sand from the desert,
acted like it wouldn't matter.
So much of want is the simple act
of leaving something out.

False Start

In shallow water
the tree finds a way
to adapt. Too much
of any one thing
feels like an open oven,
heating the kitchen
but dissipating
into the cold air. I think
silence and the morning
answers back. Funny
how so much
of blame is blunt
interaction. A forest
one day will intersect
this house—
a Carolina wren
will perch in this room.

On Pestilence

—after Maya C. Popa

The idea of continuity continues to be unclear,
turning one page to another as if the globe
isn't in flames or careening off course into dust,
singed despite minor personal destructions. I sing
a moment from fact to omen, from omen to a less formal
lie, think of the days charged with some electricity
that no one can name. We should remain animals
in this way, resisting one foot in the room
and the other in a room built to resemble
a world with no exits. The floorboards
creak disbelievingly. Did they say a word
or a sentence wide enough to contain what's left
of hope? Completely undone, the animals
object to nothing, but we all know the truth,
how the blindness of staring into the sun
is a mistake only humans will make. A possum
crawls out to the street. Everyone's
too busy looking up to notice it standing there.

The Cemetery Where My Grandparents Are Buried

When my grandparents bought these plots,
the property was on the outskirts
of town, and they couldn't have known
what a piece of land would
be surrounded by a half-century
from where they stood. My parents take flowers.
Later that day in passing, they mention
a Veterans Cemetery in the middle
of the state, remotely distant
but kept up by law. Perhaps they'll
choose this space. I think of making
plans. I think of Michael
and how Valerie flew home early
from their vacation and died
later that night in her sleep. What
did she know then that he couldn't
have understood? In that year there
could be no funeral, no gatherings. What
can it mean to leave the door of closure
wide open? Every part of a day becomes
a part of us like how in the darkest corner
of a house, thunder finds its way inside.

Diagnostic Mess

Memories of pollen in the gutter.
A childhood three turns
from today. I can't silence
this TV. Some hotel-like hell. Your
face in the mirror—too bright
of a light. I drop an O
into the soup, despite
what the recipe says, and suddenly
it makes a sentence in the dark.

On the Day When No One Was Born

Smoke rolls through
the voices singing *happy birthday*
to you, but it's not your birthday
or a day for any birth,
really. Where will regret
go at the end of the story? It is
only a piece of the puzzle
we'll call your life. Always
we find new ways to be troubled,
but there might be a rough
circling to the self
reflected in the eye of the other
self you lost. This state
is strange, and this state
of being is stranger,
but eventually it will be
your birthday and what will
you say to the singing, to the cake
lowered slowly from a helicopter?
Nothing's random. An ending
like a salmon swimming off.

Grief in a Time of Warming

My phone lights up with a weather warning.
My phone lights up with an air quality warning.
My phone lights up with news of another
friend's death. Michael writes me later
in the day, tells me these messages will only
become more common as we, and if we,
grow older. I dream of cemeteries
forever void of mourners, grocery carts filling
the oceans, and pieces of the sky falling
like puzzle parts big enough for a school of birds
to fly right through. Last week, Michael
and his children packed up their belongings
and moved south to a city that will likely
be underwater in a century. A river
can be stepped over where it begins,
but at the gulf, it becomes so wide
it can pull a living thing under with indifference
that somehow feels generous. Each day
I'm surprised by how grief finds me, like how
the trees from my childhood loom larger
in memory when I return to their branches
in this present and fleeting life.

Certain

This trip / around the sun / is expensive.

—Peter Gizzi

Are you mad at me, I ask
myself in sleep. Some
footsteps land softer
than others. Where my
legs take me, my mind
doesn't imagine negative
capability driving me right into
the ditch of good fortune.
A debt of thought always
weighs the river down.

You Can't Be Against Forever

—from David Berman

The birds circle overhead
to gauge the odds they'll
eat today while I think of Merwin
passing the anniversary of his death
so many times. I do the math
and step outside. The day could
be almost done, but what of the chance
encounters we miss by locking
the deadbolt and checking it throughout
the night? Once I sat in a coffee shop
as a car drove through the building,
sending a refrigerator across
the room. *Thank god no one was hurt*
fills the awkward space. The next day
everyone who had been sitting
feet from the refrigerator decided
to wake up and try living out their life
some other way. Some forgot
gradually. Others eventually. The world
always returns to its dull gleam.

Eternal Things

I realized I never wrote a poem
about Italy. My daughter
rock-hounding with a Russian woman
who didn't speak English. Dreamt
of eating mussels every night. Sea tomatoes
in a cave—a missed reservation. I realized
I never wrote a poem about a lot of things.
The world is ending, and we're priced out
of what we need. A cloud this morning
nearly knocked me down. In 2020
I mostly stopped reading. When
routines become abandoned, a train
continually cuts this town in half.
What side will you be on? Penny
and I drove to Santa Fe.
Sunflowers stretched their petals
three hundred and sixty degrees.
The sun was everywhere.
I felt my skin burning
on a short walk around the block.
An elegy can be anything.
An elegy can be a soup recipe.
Mathias and I sat on the front porch
in April that year and watched the sky
split in half. Poets in crossword puzzles
like skulls on the mantle. I apologize
for the state I live in. I take communion,

it brings Kathy to tears. *Tears* is a word
I usually don't use in poems.
I stumble over what should be simple.
Everything can be misread.
I don't want to forget the woman
on the plane whose son died three weeks before.
He went for a walk and didn't come back.
I write them into this poem like it can change anything.
Every muscle aches toward a word.
I fall in love as the world turns to ruin.

3.

Structures of Living

What's compatible with structures
on this side of living? The combination
of words like some bell
for a door that won't
open. I'm talking about a literal door,
my grandmother's voice
still off in the wings: *I don't love you,*
but she did. Also she would say:
I'm going to put you in the briar patch.
Not just *any* briar patch,
mind you. Everything's holy
to those in heaven.

Strange Animal Facts

I read about a species of ant that crawls
into electronics to feed on the wiring
and ultimately electrocutes itself. Upon
dying, the ant releases a chemical
calling other ants to avenge its death. I shake
my phone in the early mornings
to wake up alongside me. I walk through
the hallway of my house and think
nothing of the mechanics
of my body. I started crying yesterday
because of a single note in a song
that was mostly unremarkable
up until that moment. Later, I poured
myself down the drain with the water
I take every night habitually and ritually
to place on the nightstand and never drink.
I divide the day up into parts that make sense,
but it's all meaningless to the trees growing
always for a life beyond my own. I sleep
under a blanket that resists the movement
of my body. I arrange my day
around the unnecessary and the good.

Polaroid Elegy

The lines I steer between waking
blur solidly in sleep. Sometimes
in that world the dead
had never died, but other times
they were never here; rather
they're some outdated
sketch turned to a painting
left in a room dusty from
lack of passing through. How
not to internalize grief's
strange circle? I miss
the days when even
a shut-eye photo
felt precious for lack
of quantity. I have a box
of photos stashed away
I love for its finite
dimensions I could set
on fire and destroy. In one
candid moment from some
year unknown, the look
on my face like a cross
between a sneeze and being
carried off to another world.

Historically Windy Locations

On this side of loss
it seems more honest to blame
the spark of an outdated
electrical system than
the chemicals and cells
we call feelings on a good
day. The heart shouldn't
flutter when you're sitting
still, I hear someone say
two tables over,
but the heart is its own
mess of wonder and blood
caring not for real estate
or weather systems
as a heartbeat patterns
a life into shapes and stretched
borders. I had a dream
my dreams didn't matter,
cleaning broken glass
and so focused on
the mess, I didn't realize
my feet had caught fire.

Eventually One Point Where We Arrive

Enough has been written about birds,
about the loons somewhere on the lake
drifting out of the eye's grasp so far
from their calls that they shift
into two different birds: their actual form
while in another they become
the ideal version of what a bird
should be. Enough has been written
about the curiosity of a child who
asks why the birds landing in the backyard
skitter away when we come near, the question
difficult beneath its asking yet simple as glass
on glass on its surface. Enough, too,
have the poets written about old age, about
the mirror and its illuminated shortcomings.
Enough has been said about the inevitability
of closure in all things: endings sometimes
too much to imagine, while for others birth
may take years, those affected by concentric circles
long since gone beyond the space they once
inhabited (one hopes) into a different mirror,
though they are all the same reflections,
carrying the glare of the eyes that have come before
them with such ease, with a chisel for a stone,
a promise deep within its geologic folds.

Facing the Wrong Way

I tend to beginnings
with woodstoves of ash,
swerve from traffic
to find myself
stunned by clouds
suspended in the left lane. I can
almost recall the exact feel
of my body against
the seat, traveling backwards,
placing what I've made
on earth in the hands
of a stranger pulling levers,
avoiding danger
depending on the day. All
of my shadows piled up
amount to nothing
in all honesty like
how mulch means less
than the sum of its trees.

Blessedness Is Ours

Picking myself up from bed and into news of last night's noise from the loop of rootless trees, I find a thread of promise in the words of Darwish, something to bring less helplessness: *almond trees have illuminated the footprints of passersby.* Four egrets align in the mind, and this vision burns so clear it cannot be a memory on the border of a siege or even a siege itself. What does it mean to drift free of thought or within a thought? *In consequence of currents,* sensory and the desire to feel tells us less of the magnitude and more about the risk of water without land or an ocean slight enough to mirror the sky's shallow ridge. When thoughts arrive they seem pristine on the face or as if *swift* means *certain.* On second or third thought, they are more like what a silo holds: layers upon layers of history and danger in the way of resistance toward a simple way of thinking: describe the light of early morning as a bruise? No need to. The day mirrors without us, lifting up and out like a spruce.

Collegiality Statement

An idea torn from the mind
becomes some sentence
discarded, better off dead
than expressed. One can
say anything out loud,
and some people do. Where's
the knob to pull that'll
unravel the day? One
can't even really say
good fences anymore
as of late, but we're
all thinking it. Someone
says it. *I think you're muted*
becomes *please mute
yourself.* I iron a shirt
while we vote on it.

Some Internal Aura

The gulf turns its gears
deeper into woodgrain,
stirring up what the sun
left behind. I always anticipate
stars where they shouldn't be
and don't question
the road blurred and blurring
still. Probably a return
on an investment, a response
from some cosmic turning,
like native plants dug up
just to destroy something. Some
driving force shapes time
into a container so small
I stun myself awake from even
the deepest corners of sleep.

Figures into Darkness

> What a good / human life / looks like.
>
> —Forrest Gander

Not sure the opposite
of loss really figures
into darkness,
but we need both sides
of a life to see it whole,
its perfect arc
bending out again
through the daylight.

You're Not a Bee

—Arkansas Department of Transportation

You see two stone white cranes
flying over a drainage ditch
in love not with each other
but with the idea of being birds
born for some other world
and placed here for a purpose
beyond their knowing.

In Place of a Nap

> Not this dividing and indifferent blue.
>
> —Wallace Stevens

Salted fruit in bed
where a day turns
into a dozen like they
always have and always
should. Sunday
afternoon blurs with
the morning, no rug
on the floor, but the blue
of the sky is a canopy
to catch and hold
the word *why*.

In a Silent Way

The wounded deer
died in the impossible
garden. Did it become
the orchid that shouldn't
be there, the cactus thriving
in a rain puddle? The trestle
bridge carries more weight
than my body, but the heft
of a memory changes
all things. I look between
the cracks in words for a place
that will hold water,
a place sand can fill in
with temporary glass. An owl
I love for its elusiveness,
as if it was always there
in the tree, so still its falsity
eclipses the call. The world
isn't prone to forgive imagined
thought, but eventually
all light decides to acquiesce.
I turn all aspirations into
driftwood and sandstone.
The wounded deer dies
in the impossible garden,
but a word made it resurrect
itself into perfectly honed

light. What reflects the self
back to the self isn't eternal
or a finite ending. I left
the flower that made me
think of you for another day—
it's still deep in the woods
of my memory, holding
this world in place.

Self-Portrait at Forty-One

Through a blank slate
of feelings, I ran miles
wondering if it had rained
or if it was dew on the grass
when I stepped out to light
this morning. How to know
when I'll feel like my old self
or maybe life's just a click
of urge and want, the buzz
of an airplane I heard and a stalk
of bamboo split near some
graffiti unreadable. I'd like
to remember today
even though it felt ordinary
and gray. Some unnamed purple
patch of wildflowers. The mystery
of everything sudden.

Settlement

I used to follow each branch
of every tree down to its
trunk. Some made sense. Some
followed a line like a day gone
bad. It turns out
you can be miserable so long
you fall in love with
the feeling. What's easier: grieving
in small bouts daily or holding
out until colors call
out for new names? I chose
the former but didn't know I had.
I didn't know until I walked
out of the courthouse
that perfect day
in August. I marked time with each
breath, looking endlessly forward
to the next. I took a walk
with my daughter that day,
took a picture of a flower
anyone else might call a weed.

What I Pray For

A dumpster filled with soil and rosemary
dropped from the sky, a portable
Earth Room. Born from a sentence meant
for another world, what makes
sense is always a touch more subtle. Sleep
habits disrupted by a car wreck
I didn't see. The grocery store lost power,
and the freezers froze even deeper over
night. Where in space are we or should we be?
I remember the day I watered the garden,
and from the dirt a dozen birds flew out.

ACKNOWLEDGMENTS

Poems from this collection have appeared in *Annulet, A Public Space, Bennington Review, Cream City Review, Cherry Tree, Descant, Diode, Green Mountains Review, Harp & Altar, Laurel Review, Mid/South Sonnets: A Belle Point Press Anthology, Ninth Letter, Oversound, Poet's Country, Thrush, The Slowdown, Well Poetry Review,* and *You Are Here: Poetry in the Natural World.*

I am grateful to everyone at Milkweed Editions for their support and generosity. Thank you especially to Daniel Slager, Shannon Blackmer, Joanna Demkiewicz, Mary Austin Speaker, Jaye Elizabeth Elijah, and Bailey Hutchinson.

My thanks also to Mathias Svalina, Shannon Jonas, Ada Limón, Michael Robins, Tracy Zeman, Monika Gehlawat, Joshua Bernstein, Brody Parrish Craig, Natalie Shapero, Samantha Clare, and Penny Clay.

ADAM CLAY is the author of four collections of poems: *To Make Room for the Sea*, *Stranger*, *A Hotel Lobby at the Edge of the World*, and *The Wash*. His poems have appeared in *Tin House*, *Ploughshares*, *Denver Quarterly*, *Georgia Review*, *Crazyhorse*, *Bennington Review*, and *jubilat*, and online at Poetry Daily and the Poem-a-Day project of the Academy of American Poets. He is editor of *Mississippi Review* and teaches in the Center for Writers at the University of Southern Mississippi.

milkweed
EDITIONS

Founded as a nonprofit organization in 1980, Milkweed Editions is an independent publisher. Our mission is to identify, nurture, and publish transformative literature and build an engaged community around it.

Milkweed Editions is based in Bdé Óta Othúŋwe (Minneapolis) within Mní Sota Makhóče, the traditional homeland of the Dakhóta people. Residing here since time immemorial, Dakhóta people still call Mní Sota Makhóče home, with four federally recognized Dakhóta nations and many more Dakhóta people residing in what is now the state of Minnesota. Due to continued legacies of colonization, genocide, and forced removal, generations of Dakhóta people remain disenfranchised from their traditional homeland. Presently, Mní Sota Makhóče has become a refuge and home for many Indigenous nations and peoples, including seven federally recognized Ojibwe nations. We humbly encourage our readers to reflect upon the historical legacies held in the lands they occupy.

milkweed.org

Milkweed Editions, an independent nonprofit publisher, gratefully acknowledges sustaining support from our Board of Directors; the Alan B. Slifka Foundation and its president, Riva Ariella Ritvo-Slifka; the Amazon Literary Partnership; *Copper Nickel*; the McKnight Foundation; the National Endowment for the Arts; the National Poetry Series; and other generous contributions from foundations, corporations, and individuals. Also, this activity is made possible by the voters of Minnesota through a Minnesota State Arts Board Operating Support grant, thanks to a legislative appropriation from the arts and cultural heritage fund. For a full listing of Milkweed Editions supporters, please visit milkweed.org.

Interior design by Zoe Norvell
Typeset in Adobe Caslon Pro

Adobe Caslon Pro is a classic serif typeface with roots dating
back to the 18th century. It was designed by William Caslon in
England. The digital version, Adobe Caslon Pro, was developed
by Carol Twombly in 1990, preserving the elegant characteristics
of the original while offering enhanced legibility and versatility
for modern digital applications.